W9-AWV-214

Joan Hewett

TUNNELS, TRACKS, and TRAINS

BUILDING A SUBWAY

PHOTOGRAPHS BY **Richard Hewett**

HOUGHTON MIFFLIN   BOSTON • MORRIS PLAINS, NJ

California • Colorado • Georgia • Illinois • New Jersey • Texas

to Rosemary Brosnan, for caring

Editor: Rosemary Brosnan   Designer: Barbara Powderly

Tunnels, Tracks, and Trains: Building a Subway, by Joan Hewett, photographs by Richard Hewett. Text copyright © 1995 by Joan Hewett. Photographs copyright © 1995 by Richard Hewett. Reprinted by permission of Penguin Putnam, Inc.

Houghton Mifflin Edition, 2001

No part of this work may be reproduced or transmitted in any form or by any means, electronic or mechanical, including photocopying and recording, or by any information storage or retrieval system without the prior written permission of the copyright owner unless such copying is expressly permitted by federal copyright law. With the exception of nonprofit transcription in Braille, Houghton Mifflin is not authorized to grant permission for further uses of this work. Permission must be obtained from the individual copyright owner as identified herein.

Printed in the U.S.A.

ISBN: 0-618-05991-1

23456789-B-06 05 04 03 02 01 00

ACKNOWLEDGMENTS

Our thanks to the people at Los Angeles County's Rail Construction Corporation, who helped make this book possible. We are particularly grateful to John Adams, who so generously took valuable time to explain subway construction, arrange for photographic access, and review the manuscript for technical accuracy. Special thanks also go to Jessica Cusick for her all-out cooperation and to Laurene Lopez, Dave Pollard, and Bill Mooney for answering our constant "when and where" questions.

The fascinating people we interviewed and photographed made this project a joy. Gratitude to Jack Bowling, Kathryn Lim, Roberta Greenwood, Bryan Lee, Ken Shah, Lynn Martindale, Kirk Davis, Lavonne Stuber, and artists Francisco Letelier and Thomas Eatherton. Thanks to Don Jim and Chris Hewett for photographic assistance.

LOS ANGELES IS GETTING A SUBWAY

DANGER. Signs warn pedestrians to stay clear of construction. Jackhammering jolts the air. Massive backhoes, towering cranes, workers shoveling and measuring—construction crews are everywhere—downtown, midtown, and below the town! Los Angeles is getting a subway.

Big foreign cities like Moscow, Paris, Berlin, Tokyo, Mexico City, and London have subways. Boston has this country's earliest subway system; New York has the longest. There are undergrounds in Philadelphia, Chicago, San Francisco, Miami, Atlanta, and Washington, D.C.

Although city dwellers around the world ride subways, many people in Los Angeles find the idea strange. They are used to going everywhere by car.

But the city is quickly becoming more densely populated, the freeways and streets more traffic-clogged.

Subways ease traffic problems. They speed under a city, carry large numbers of people, and they don't pollute the air. And as two recent California earthquakes have shown, properly built subways can withstand major temblors.

Los Angeles' subway, the 17.5-mile Metro Red Line, will take close to twenty years to complete. Connecting with surface rail lines, the Red Line will be the heart of the city's rapid transit system. Like all subways, it's being built segment by segment.

This book looks at one and a half years in the making of a subway, when construction has been in progress for four years and the first segment is partially completed. Work on the second segment is about to start, and the next is in the planning stage.

CHIEF CONSTRUCTION
ENGINEER, JOHN ADAMS

A special county agency oversees the building of the subway. John Adams is their vice-president in charge of overall planning and construction. Private engineering companies do a great deal of the work. John Adams' inspectors monitor construction, and John resolves problems as they arise.

John's interest in engineering goes way back. His dad was an ironworker who helped build the New York City subway. When John was a child, he listened to his dad's account of that "city under a city" and became curious about how things were built. Later, he went to college and studied engineering.

Now, John has crossed the country engineering new subway systems and new sections of existing lines. A subway buff, he collects historic photographs and prints of nineteenth-century steam-driven subways. But most of all, John enjoys the day-by-day challenge of building.

Metro Red Line's first segment runs under the city's downtown civic and financial districts. Tunnels have been bored, and four of the five planned stations have been built. John is currently concentrating on the remaining station. Construction is about to start.

AN ARCHAEOLOGICAL DIG
HALTS CONSTRUCTION

Like the other stations, Union Station will be built by "cut and cover" construction. A wide trench called a cut will be dug, the station will be built in the cut, and then the surrounding space will be filled in and covered. To hold back the soil and keep it from falling into the cut, a temporary sixty-foot-deep wall is constructed.

Once the wall is secure, digging begins. Excavation usually continues until the base of the cut is reached. But a field of artifacts lies buried here. During the boom years of long-distance travel, Old Chinatown was bulldozed to make room for a huge railroad station. Union Subway Station is being constructed on a part of the site that was cleared, but never used.

Archaeologist Roberta Greenwood will oversee preservation of the valuable artifacts. She made plans based on what she learned about the once thriving town, and has a team of archaeologists ready to assist her.

At fourteen feet below street level, digging on the cut is halted. The archaeologists fan out over the site. Roberta says, "The town was settled by Chinese men who came to the United States to work on the railroads. Later, they were joined by their families, and the population swelled. This will be a large find. Our work is just starting!"

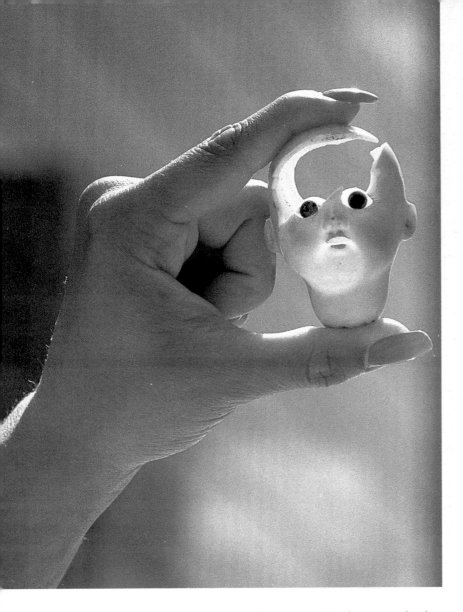

dominoes, and rusted Chinese coins. From these objects, experts will be able to tell a lot about the lives, including even the diets, of the town's inhabitants.

As soon as the archaeological dig ends, operators climb back into the cabs of their backhoes. Work on the subway station is once again under way.

For a month and a half, archaeologists comb the area. Thousands of artifacts emerge. Practical objects like spoons, teapots, steamers, toothbrushes, and a spittoon are found. There are parts of porcelain dolls, marbles in varied hues, gambling

A PARK MAKES A PERFECT CONSTRUCTION SITE

Meanwhile, construction on the subway's second segment is starting. The lake and green lawns of MacArthur Park are about to be transformed. For the next two years, the park will be a hub of Metro Red Line activity.

Workers will build cut and cover tunnels and a siding, tracks that enable a train to change direction. They will install a transformer center that boosts electrical power. There will be room on the site to store construction materials and equipment and to assemble a giant tunnel-boring machine. Because there are no close neighbors who would be disturbed, work can go on around the clock.

But first, the lake has to be drained. To keep people from harm's way, a high chain link fence is erected around the park, and signs about the upcoming subway are posted. Park employees round up the lake's ducks and geese and move them to another city lake. Eighty trees are uprooted, planted in temporary containers, and set around the park's edge.

After this section of the subway is completed, the park will be reconstructed: Trees will be replanted, lawns reseeded, paths paved, a new lake built, and ducks and geese returned. Meanwhile, brightly colored paintings by neighborhood artists are hung around the fence.

As the water recedes, baseballs, shopping carts, bottles, cans, and other objects that have sunk to the lake's bottom begin to appear. After two months, all of the water—23 million gallons—has been pumped.

But construction still cannot start. Soil tests show a low level of contamination. Chemicals to purify the lake's water have seeped into the earth. For several weeks, the dank earth is loaded onto dump trucks and taken to a specially lined landfill.

Then, the enormous, sixty-foot-deep, sixty-foot-wide cut is under way. Carrying equipment and consulting drawings, surveyors, people skilled in the art of measuring, target points where the earth will be reinforced. Stopping at these points, tractors equipped with augers, rotating corkscrew-like cutting blades, pull up dirt and dig narrow holes into the base of the cut. Steel beams are dropped in, and the holes are "poured up" with concrete. Later, wooden piles set between the beams complete the reinforcing.

A permanent concrete wall will support the excavation and serve as the tunnel's outer wall. Almost as tall as a six-story building, it's reinforced by eighty-foot-long soldier beams, vertical beams in an evenly spaced line, anchored into the base of the cut. Then, the contour of the wall is formed around the vertical beams, and the first layer of concrete is poured.

15

PROJECT MANAGER BRYAN LEE

To Project Manager Bryan Lee, the surging activity is a wonderful sight. The job's on track.

Employed by a construction company that has a contract to build this section of the subway, Bryan makes sure that the terms of the contract are carried out. He has many concerns. Do building methods and materials match those in the agreement? Are schedules met? Are costs kept within bounds?

Field engineers, who monitor construction, safety engineers, who check working conditions, and other experts report directly to Bryan. Still, when Bryan's not problem solving or going over facts and figures, he likes to leave his desk and see what's going on.

Bryan's been engineering subways for eighteen years. "Not many people build subways, so we're in demand," Bryan says. "And when you move on to another job in a different city, there are always men and women aboard who you've worked with before. It's a special kind of camaraderie. I like that."

HAULING THE DIRT AWAY

Excavation at the park continues for several months. Wearing hard hats and protective steel-toed boots, supervisors, foremen, surveyors, inspectors, steel workers, and laborers report for work early in the morning. Lines of dump trucks rumbling down a makeshift dirt road blow clouds of dust into the air.

Thirty to fifty large dump trucks converge on the site each day. Hauling hills of newly dug dirt is a major operation. Skilled front-end loader operators fill a truck with fifteen cubic yards of dirt in two minutes! The trucks make two round-trips daily, from the park to the dump and back again.

Finally, the base of the cut is reached. An initial layer of concrete reinforces the base, and it's time for tunnel boring to start.

THE MIGHTY BORING MACHINE IS ASSEMBLED

From the park on, the subway route goes under busy midtown Los Angeles. Boring creates far less surface disturbance than cut and cover construction. So, like the downtown tunnels, these tunnels will be bored.

From his bird's-eye-view office, engineer Ken

Shah watches the arrival of the massive, gleaming, 180-foot-long tunnel-boring machine. It will be lowered piece by piece and assembled on the excavation's floor.

Savoring the moment, miners, the men who will operate the boring machine, watch and wait. A crane swings into sight, aligns the boring machine's cutting rim with the proposed tunnel, and sets it down.

The machine consists of a front section, or shield, and a long, trailing back section. The shield does the boring. Driven by electricity, the shield's hydraulically powered pistons can bring six thousand pounds of pressure against the earth. Its mechanical arm, which has a scoop on one side and a pick on the other, digs, pulls down, and shovels muck, dirt excavated from a tunnel, onto a conveyor belt.

The long, trailing back section has two levels. One supports the conveyor belt; the other holds big air ducts. Powerful fans suck stagnant tunnel air through these ducts and out of the tunnel. As the foul air departs, fresh air rushes in.

Some soil has high levels of harmful gases. To protect people's health, the shield has a built-in gas detector, and each miner wears a belt equipped with an oxygen mask and a short, lifesaving supply of oxygen.

TUNNELING AND JACK BOWLING, A MINER'S MINER

Two teams of miners operate the machine. Each works an eight-hour shift. The work is grueling and potentially dangerous. Most of the twelve to thirteen men on a team know one another well. They have mined together, relied on one another, and stayed the course. Their helmets sport stickers, trophies from other tunnels they have bored.

Jack Bowling is proud to be a miner. As "walking boss," he strikes the pace for the men on his team, who install tunnel lining and tracks and run the conveyor belt and muck carts.

Before this job, Jack mined subway tunnels in Atlanta and San Francisco. His family travels with him. Jack's dad and granddad mined tunnels. "They used dynamite a lot more then," Jack says regretfully, as though some of the old derring-do has disappeared.

Lining up and testing the boring machine takes several days. Then, it's time to start. The miners are eager and tense. Two men sit up front. One operates the hydraulic driving-cutting gear and, with the help of a laser, keeps the shield on course. The other operates the digging arm.

Progress is slow at first. The soil is rocky. A heavy, continuous rain overloads the tunnel pumping system. But team members find their rhythm, and the shield is soon advancing thirty feet or more each day.

Vibrating mightily, the mechanized mole moves forward, up, down, and to the sides, creating a 24-foot-diameter hole. To keep the hole from collapsing, it is lined with precast cement rings. The rings come in sections. As the shield advances, miners stationed in the rear of the shield use mechanical erector arms to help haul and shove the heavy sections into place.

Meanwhile, other miners put down more track, so trains can carry the muck from the trailer's conveyor belt to the outside. A locomotive pushes four empty carts and a flatbed bearing cement rings into the tunnel. But the muck is so heavy that it takes two locomotives to move the filled carts.

Throughout the night, specially installed lights cast an eerie glow over the open excavation. Grime-encrusted locomotives come to a stop, special carts mechanically dump the muck onto a long conveyor belt, and the slow-moving, click-clacking belt carries it up out of the pit.

At 6:00 A.M., miners and an occasional gas or safety inspector finish their night shifts and make their way up the steep iron staircase. As they check out, the next shift checks in.

PLASTIC LININGS AND STEEL BEAMS

Only yards away, a tough, waterproof plastic lining has been rolled out over the cut and cover construction. Now, walking on steel beams, sure-footed laborers reinforce walls and floor with a cagelike steel grid. Then, a thick layer of poured concrete seals the cut and forms the tunnel's "mud slab" floor.

READYING SURFACE STREETS

Meanwhile, other construction crews have been getting the Red Line's midtown route ready for boring. They reinforce foundations of buildings along the route and secure electric, gas, water, and telephone lines that run beneath the street.

27

Some lines that might be damaged are fed into pipes along the side of the road. Crews work on one side of the street at a time. That way, only one lane is closed, and traffic can keep rolling.

To keep traffic moving while cut and cover stations are being constructed, a temporary road called decking is built over the torn-up streets. During the night, while the area is largely deserted, streets are closed off. Steel beams that span the cut's width are set down, and sets of attached wooden beams are placed between them. This makes a strong, solid surface, but one that can be quickly converted. The wooden sections are designed to be lifted out. Machinery can be lowered through the opening to the floor of the cut.

KATHRYN LIM DESIGNS SUBWAY STATIONS

The subway stations are far more than a place for people to get on and off trains. Kathryn Lim, who heads the county's subway station design team, says, "We're creating unique underground environments. We want to build functional stations that people will enjoy."

Even when Kathryn was an architecture student, she knew she wanted to design public places. "If you plan a home for a family and the entire

size that do not make people feel dwarfed takes a sense of scale.

When Kathryn was a child, she loved making small paper constructions. Some were like tiny buildings. Now, despite computer software programs that bring a three-dimensional look to architectural drawings, Kathryn still constructs models. She says, "A model doesn't just seem three-dimensional; it is. And when you add lights and figures cut to scale, it comes alive! You start to see what it's like inside."

Once Kathryn and her team complete a concept and develop guidelines, the actual design job goes to a private architectural firm, and Kathryn turns to new challenges.

family enjoys it, well, that's nice," Kathryn says. "But creating an environment for a great many people seems more challenging and more worthwhile."

Some stations are the length of a fifty-story-high building lying on its side. Others are as long as an eighty-story building! To design stations this

FINISHING WORK

While the subway's second segment is in the early construction stage, the last stages of work go forward on the first segment. Cables that carry electric power and pipes that bring in water, in case of fire, are installed along the tunnel walls. A narrow concrete walkway is built along the sides. In an emergency, passengers could use it to reach the nearest station.

Things have to be done in order. Pumps to suck underground water and collected rainwater from the tunnels are secured before the special platform for train rails is anchored into place. And before this is done, surveyors make sure the platform follows the exact line laid out by the engineer.

The trains will be powered by a third rail that carries electricity. Because busy workers might accidentally step on this "hot rail," it's not installed until the tunnel is almost operational.

In the stations, the sounds of drilling, sawing, and hammering fill the air as carpenters, welders, tile layers, and electricians complete their tasks. Huge ventilating fans keep fresh air flowing, and gas inspectors equipped with hand-held meters regularly check the quality of the air. Permanent gas- and fire-detecting machines with built-in alarm systems will be installed shortly.

A flatbed truck known as the "Pink Lady" brings materials and fixtures to the workers. Above ground, the specially outfitted truck looks like any truck that happens to be bright pink. Then, driver Lynn Martindale lowers the truck's train wheels, and sounding its "get out of the way" horn, she steers the Pink Lady through the tunnels.

Lynn enjoys her job. She says, "It's kind of unique. I've delivered everything, from countless sacks of cement, to steel frames, to a station escalator that just fit into the flatbed."

SUBWAY ART

In the midst of all the building, artists put final touches on, or help install, their artwork. Each station's art reflects the character or history of its particular neighborhood. And throughout the subway, different kinds of work are featured: neon art installations, hanging fiberglass sculptures, murals painted in varying styles.

Francisco Letelier is one of several artists who submitted ideas for the Art for Rail Transit Program. Known for his murals, Francisco had never done one in tile. Still, he felt that tile seemed right for this project. So Francisco learned how to plan and execute a tile mural and, after patient experimentation, how to make his own tiles. Then, he thought about themes, sketched his ideas, and submitted them.

The young Chilean-born painter was commissioned to create two large murals, "The Sun" and "The Moon," for the Westlake–MacArthur Park station. He has worked on this giant project one mural at a time: painting tiles, numbering and lettering them on the back so he knows where they will go, and then firing them in his kiln.

Now, more than a year after he officially started, Francisco is overseeing the installation of his creation.

Thomas Eatherton's "sleight of eye" light work will not be found in any station. The fiber-optic panels are installed along the walls of a tunnel. Tiny lights set in the panels form fixed abstract patterns. But when passengers on a passing train see the

work, the patterns will seem to change.

CENTRAL CONTROL

Behind the scenes, new technology makes it possible for Metro Central Control to watch over the entire rail system.

Trains are tracked by a specially designed computer—fiber-optic system. Housed in minute boxes attached to the rails, computer chips sense each train's location and speed. Connecting fiber-optic lines almost instantaneously relay the information to central control computers. Computer operators "see" and follow the train's progress on

their screens. Using automatic signaling and track switching systems, traffic can be regulated, and if need be, rerouted.

Individual train operators and central control are linked by police-type radios and silent alarms. In turn, central control and police and fire stations are linked by direct phone lines. A special police unit housed in the control center could quickly move to an emergency site.

The center also oversees subway station security. TV cameras installed throughout the stations relay images to banks of TV sets that monitor the different areas. Operators scan the screens looking for people who need help and those who might cause trouble. They can talk to people in the stations over a public-address system or use walkie-talkies to alert roaming security guards.

A thief who has pickpocketed a wallet without seeming to attract attention might be apprehended minutes later. People leaning over the tracks might be jolted by a booming voice warning them to stay back.

THE BORING MACHINE
BREAKS THROUGH

Out of sight of electronic security, the boring machine presses forward. As they near their goal— the first midtown station—the miners on each shift work a little harder and move a little faster.

Construction workers reinforce the rough cut and cover station with steel girders. In the station, they can hear a distant rumbling noise. The earth shakes, the mighty boring machine breaks into the station, and the miners give a rousing cheer.

Boring the 7,166-foot tunnel has taken two and a half months, somewhat longer than estimated. Dirt and rocks have dulled the once shiny machine. But for Jack Bowling and the other miners, it's time to celebrate and rest. The machine will be over-hauled. Problems that slowed boring have been solved. The men are sure that the next tunnel can be bored much faster, and time proves them right.

HERE COME THE TRAINS

TV, radio, and newspapers spread the news: The first subway segment is scheduled to open in a few months.

At the Metro rail yard, Kirk Davis and the other Red Line train operators are delighted. The high-tech subway cars have finally arrived!

It took many months for the first train to be tested for safety, performance, and endurance. Then, engineering and design changes were made before production on the trains began. The process was slow.

To gain experience, operators have been driving similar trains, leased from the Miami, Florida, subway system. Even so, they are eager to drive and become familiar with the workings of their "own" cars.

A special shoe at the bottom of the car collects electricity from the third rail. This electricity powers the motor. When a train slows to a stop, it doesn't use much power, so the surplus electricity is stored. The train's braking system pumps it into an on-board generator. Starting takes extra power. The stored electricity creates the electrical surge that's needed to pick up speed.

Sitting behind the control board, Kirk turns on the motor, pulls back on the throttle, and, accelerating smoothly, drives the new train along the train yard tracks. Kirk was a city bus driver. To become a train operator, he had to pass a physical examination that proved he was healthy and a written exam that showed he could understand and retain information as well as make sound decisions.

Now, the time has come to put the new trains through their paces. At night, when the construction workers have gone, the first Red Line train whizzes through the gleaming tunnels, past Thomas Eatherton's fiber-optic art, and through the lofty, silent stations.

Los Angeles is getting a subway and it's coming soon!

When some years have passed and subway trains link residential and business areas, people in Los Angeles will have forgotten that an underground transit system ever seemed like an odd idea. The subway will be part of city life.

And by then, Jack Bowling, John Adams, Bryan Lee, Kathryn Lim, and some of the other people you've read about in this book may be in different cities, creating new and wondrous subterranean complexes.

INDEX